SMALL FRIENDS

and other stories and poems

SMALL FRIENDS

and other stories and poems

by students of

King George VI
School and Centre

'amaBooks

ISBN 978-0-7974-9452-7
EAN 9780797494527

Published by 'amaBooks
P.O. Box AC1066, Ascot, Bulawayo
amabooksbyo@gmail.com
www.amabooksbyo.com

Cover Design: Veena Bhana
based on a painting by Sininisabo Tshuma

This publication is a result of a collaboration between the United States'
President's Emergency Plan For Aids Relief (PEPFAR), King George VI
School and Centre for Physically Disabled Children and 'amaBooks
Publishers.

'amaBooks would particularly like to thank Jillian Bonnardeaux of the
Embassy of the United States of America to Zimbabwe and Inez Hussey,
Marvelous Mbulo, the staff and the students of King George VI for making
this publication possible.

Contents

Introduction

It is a pleasure for me to introduce this collection of short stories and poems, *Small Friends*, written by students at King George VI School and Centre for Children with Physical Disabilities (KGVI) in Zimbabwe's second city, Bulawayo.

As the U.S. Ambassador to Zimbabwe, it is my responsibility to strengthen and enhance our relationship with the people of Zimbabwe. For decades, one of the key commitments from the American people to the people of Zimbabwe has been in the area of health diplomacy, because a healthy Zimbabwe is a priority for us. As my friends with disabilities have taught me, having a disability is not a sign of inability; it simply means that we are differently abled. My U.S. Embassy team works hard to create outreach efforts on health to ensure that vulnerable people, including those with disabilities, benefit from important health information and services.

This publication was made possible through the support of the U.S. President's Emergency Plan for AIDS Relief (PEPFAR) and the Public Affairs Section of the U.S. Embassy in Harare. PEPFAR supports the people of Zimbabwe by increasing their access to HIV prevention, care and treatment efforts, assistance to orphans and vulnerable children, strengthening of Zimbabwe's health system, and gender integration. Additionally, PEPFAR is building and strengthening the capacity of the Government of Zimbabwe through system strengthening of laboratories, informatics, human resources for health, and the quality assurance of health programs. In 2013, PEPFAR provided the people of Zimbabwe with over $95 million towards the national response to HIV and AIDS and pledged the same amount for 2014.

I am especially proud of this collection of short stories and poems because it is the result of a collaboration between the KGVI School, 'amaBooks Publishers and the U.S. Embassy. 'amaBooks and the Embassy have worked together before: on creative reading projects for young people across Bulawayo, on the provision of library facilities, and on creative writing workshops held at the Resource Centre of the Opportunistic Infections Unit at Mpilo Hospital that benefit nearly 1,500 young people living with HIV and AIDS in the city and enable these youth to find their voices through the written word.

This particular collection of stories is an example of a platform that we have created for young people with disabilities to voice their concerns and dreams; it is also a useful tool to advocate for an environment that will allow them to participate in national developmental programs. Some of the stories and poems tell the stories of their lives, some are purely fictional, and some speak of their personal dreams of a better future. I am particularly touched by the story on page four entitled 'Unfulfilled Wishes'.

HIV and AIDS have had a devastating effect in Zimbabwe. Although Zimbabwe has managed to record a significant decline in HIV prevalence, about 1.2 million children have lost one or both parents due to HIV and AIDS-related ailments. KGVI students – and people with disabilities in general – are not exempt from the impact of HIV and AIDS, a tragic reality that is reflected in many of the pieces in this collection. Indeed, several KGVI graduates have become caregivers for younger children after serious illness cut short the lives of their parents.

KGVI provides rehabilitation and boarding facilities to children with physical disabilities and hearing impairments from the age of three years to eighteen years. It is the only secondary education facility in Zimbabwe for children with disabilities and the only primary school catering to young people with special needs in the southern part of the country. That is why KGVI was a natural partner for this project. But we hope that this collection will make an impact far beyond the school's walls.

I believe that this book demonstrates both the talent of these students and their concerns about the issues facing their community and wider society, and will also serve as an advocacy tool in lobbying for improved services for vulnerable people with disabilities.

I am so pleased to have the opportunity to support this project and other projects like it, which inspire young people to contemplate their lives, their communities, their futures and express themselves in written word and verse.

D. Bruce Wharton
U.S. Ambassador to Zimbabwe

March 2014

King George VI

Abigail Ncube

Among the many schools in Zimbabwe, King George VI, opened in 1957, is special. It is a school and centre that helps physically disabled and deaf scholars realise their full potential.

King George VI has helped children with disability achieve way beyond the expectations of many people. Some of its students have excelled academically, while others have done well in areas such as sport, music and drama. While society sometimes leaves the disabled to beg in the streets, King George VI takes them in and teaches them how best to live independently. By independent living, we mean people with disability being able to do household chores such as cooking, washing and cleaning.

In educating and training its talented students in various fields, King George VI also sources scholarships for its scholars. A vibrant marimba band, a bakery, story writers and singers that sing like birds in the trees are all part of the family of King George VI.

We take pride in exceptional success stories, such as the King George VI scholars who formed the musical band Liyana. The Oscar winning film *Music by Prudence* featured the band of Prudence Mabhena, Goodwell Nzou, Energy Maburutse, Honest Mupatsi, Tapiwa Nyengera, Marvelous Mbulo, Vusani Vuma and Farai Mabhande.

From the above, you can see that the motto of the organisation 'Never Give Up' is fulfilled. The accomplishments of the students prove that disability does not mean inability. The least expected achievements at King George VI surprise and touch many.

Small Friends

Marvelous Mbulo

Summer time, life is hectic, mother, father, boys and girls, all busy. Hoeing, weeding, ploughing and sowing. Natural sounds of different tones addressing the mood of the season. As a young boy, left on a patch yet to be cultivated, questions raced through my mind. I accused God but at the same time found myself appreciating the tender love and care that my mother gave me each day. Life without her would be a nightmare. As I sat supported with stones, I admired the people around me, standing, bending, walking, and throwing; they were as busy as bees and I wondered what it was like to be under such pressure. The crowing, chirping and mooing I heard made me wonder if the animals and birds shared the same sentiments. Maybe it was just my loneliness. Maybe those in the fields were wishing they were like me spending the days seated, propped up with stones, and I wished I was like them, spending the days working in the fields from sunrise till sunset.

As I filled myself with these thoughts, not knowing what would become of me, a chameleon appeared on a low branch of a tree next to me.

'Do you want to scare me, dear creature?' I asked in a silent voice.

It looked at me and started changing colours, as if it was trying to talk to me. It turned red, 'Danger,' I thought, then green, 'That's for food,' I surmised. Next it turned brown, and I thought 'no, no, this one is for cover.' It was like the chameleon was telling me something and we, chameleon and boy, were delighted when we discovered that we could understand each other. In no time a moth appeared and my dear friend turned green and stretched his long tongue, and into his mouth went the juicy insect. I marvelled at such skill and said 'Okay, show me some more.' It looked at me as if saying 'Slow down pal.'

Around me a colony of ants seemed busy too. With a frown on my face I took a closer look, different colours started to emerge. 'Marvelous,' I said to myself. I started giving them names, the named ones disappeared and reappeared, what on earth was going on? I mused, while appreciating nature all around me. The army of ants changed direction, now up, up the tree. 'Hey, why change direction? Aren't we having fun, plus there is danger

2

there,' I tried to warn them. Up, up, sideways and down the branch they went. I looked on and my eyes met the eyes of my old friend, he was green in colour again and his eyes were full of delight as if I was the one who had brought him lunch. Using his sticky tongue, my tiny unsuspecting friends were picked off one by one. I watched and my friend chameleon paused for a moment, I thought he was saying 'hang on, there's still more.'

Giant footsteps emerged from behind, my friend chameleon turned red. 'Why change of colour, pal?' I asked. My mother had come to pick me up. I waved bye. 'See you tomorrow,' I said in silence.

What a day, well lived, plus a unique encounter. I knew it was all for me, me alone and not to be shared with anybody since no one would understand me. Tired from concentrating and assuming this was a story to nurse, I slept soundly on my mother's back.

Unfulfilled Wishes

Oleander Payarira

If only I could find a magic lamp or a shooting star to grant my wishes. If only I could say I love you just one more time.

I loved my dear mother but I took her presence for granted. I never appreciated my packed lunch, the pencil I got to replace a lost one or the warm jersey in winter.

I never knew my father but my mother made the situation normal. It was always the two of us, mother and daughter, inseparable. She would often get sick with what I thought were minor illnesses but it turned out to be AIDS. I suspect she thought I was too immature to understand, but did I not deserve to know the truth? This was the sort of question that ran through my mind when my mother got seriously sick and, this time, she never got well, but drifted to a sleep of no return. The news came as a real shock to me and I groaned and wailed as if a thunderstorm had begun.

I knew there was no more mother and daughter, nor was there anyone else. I was alone. My father's and my mother's relatives had abandoned my mother when they found out about the disease that took her life and left me a lonely orphan.

This disease has killed many and left many homeless orphans like me. AIDS has become a part of our world and a part of who we are. It is a very dangerous disease and is even more dangerous when people are not educated about it. This is one of my reasons for writing this account. Although it hurts me every time I talk about it, if I help save one life I will be very happy.

But I am Still Alive

Preferment Rupondo

I was laughed at and looked down upon by society
I was tortured and verbally abused
I was starved
But I am still alive.

When I was young they laughed at my disability
When I was young they laughed at my parents
But I am still alive.

When I was sick there was no money for medication
When I went to school there was no money for education
But I am still alive.

Some people said I was a curse
Some people said I was a punishment
Handed down by the ancestors
But I am still alive.

Gone Fishing

Miyethani Sithole

One afternoon it was too hot and sunny for comfort. To keep cool I wore my navy blue shorts and white T-shirt, and my Dad wore a blue T-shirt with brown shorts. Dad told me that he wanted to go to the river to catch some fish for our dinner. 'It could be fun,' he said, grinning.

I agreed to go with him, though I wasn't sure it would really be fun. He drove and, on the journey to the river, I saw trees and cars flashing past and people walking. When we arrived at the river we took out our fishing rods and our chairs. We saw many people who were already there and we greeted them and looked for a cool space to sit. We found a good place in a shady spot under a tree and sat down happily with our fishing rods. My father got his rod ready and I followed what he was doing. I began to realize fishing could be fun and surely it would be exciting to make a catch. As it was my first time to go on a fishing trip my heart began beating quickly, particularly when I saw others getting excited when their fishing rods started to move. When those around us had caught all the fish they wanted they left for their homes and we waved good-bye.

We remained on the riverbank, waiting and straining to see into the river as if we could spot the fish moving, but still we caught nothing. My dad snorted as I sighed, he could tell I was getting bored, but suddenly his fishing rod moved. I rubbed my eyes as it seemed unbelievable. I shook my dad's shoulder. 'What?' he said, yawning. 'Look, your fishing rod moved,' I said, shivering with excitement. He was surprised and he held onto the rod so hard in his efforts to try and hold the fish as it tried to break away. Then he shouted to himself and struggled to land the fish. I started to grin when I realized that it looked as if we would have a fish dinner that night. Eventually he pulled the fish out of the water, and it was a really big one. We were both so happy and very excited. We packed up the fish into a box and left for home.

The clouds came over and it became very dark, so Dad had to be very careful driving. It was late evening when we arrived home and met my Mom standing in front of the house. 'Hello, let me guess,' she said, grinning.

My Dad took out the box from the car and put it on the kitchen table. Mom opened the box and was surprised and very pleased to discover such a big fish. 'Fish' she said happily. 'Yes!' I said, pleased to be bringing food for dinner.

My Mom cooked the fish and it smelt so delicious that my stomach growled. When it was ready my Mom called us from the kitchen to come and eat dinner. We were so happy to eat the big fish that we had struggled so hard to catch.

Children of Africa

Precious Sibanda

They are dark in complexion
Not blank in mind
They have the African gift
They are proudly African.

Their hearts beat in tune
To the African music
Played by the power
Of their African hands
Producing vibrant tunes
From the African drums.

Their voices echo
Throughout the African jungle
Their faith so strong
They could move a thousand mountains.

As they stamp their feet in time
The dust rises and fills mother earth.
Dressed in an African way
They dance to the tune of the drums.

Tiny but Deadly

Alex Nyathi

As I was watching *World of Wildlife,* my favourite programme on TV, my mind started racing. I marvelled at the variety of creation: huge, tiny, beautiful, on fours or twos or wings, the elephant, giraffe, hippo, vulture, spider and so many more. Such different shapes, sizes, colours and behaviours. If you take time to listen and enjoy animal behaviour, you'll find it fascinating.

I started to imagine what the world would be like if elephant, giraffe, cow and rhino were to make a deal with God to give them brains to use guns and nuclear weapons to wage war against human beings. These animals have the strength, energy and power to defeat us. Inviting the cat family for the feast after the war would be the worst. What about the crawling, creeping, slithering and winged ones? This is kind of tricky as we would still be defeated as they would be too small for us to attack. Even the numbers alone would defeat us as some of these creatures reproduce in large numbers. Human beings might not win the war. Is it therefore true that the smaller the size the deadlier the creature?

Think of the war between human beings and the HIV virus. Too small to be seen with a naked eye, not armed in any way, never having received any training in nuclear weapons, but look at the havoc it has caused. The virus is too small; it sneaks into your system without being noticed. How can you fight with something that you cannot see? Too tiny to hold a gun and fight but, once the virus gets into your body, that's it – no machine or knowledge can make it leave your body.

If the virus was as big as elephant or lion we could simply build a wall but it's not that easy. No one can say here comes the enemy, let's fight back. The HIV virus is just too clever. Human beings, both old and young, can only try and control it. But eradicate it?

As I sat there thinking about this monster, my aunt, who is always on time when it comes to taking her ARVs, asked me to go and fetch her tablets and water. As an obedient child I left my seat, still wondering, and brought her the container and a glass of water. It was raining heavily outside and, as I left, she gazed at the rain.

'Thank you,' she said. 'You know what, my niece, I wish I could just stand in the rain and let the rain wash this virus out of my body.' I looked at her and handed her the tablets without comment. As I looked out I prayed to God, wanting Him to send the heavy rains capable of making my aunt's dreams come true.

A Clever Boy

Mduduzi Mlotshwa

Once upon a time there was a poor boy who lived with his parents and his aunt. The boy's name was Sam. Sam didn't like to work, and didn't do much around the house to help his family. His aunt enjoyed working and always tried to encourage Sam to help her. One day Sam's aunt said, 'Sam, please go and find some firewood so that I can start to cook our food.' Sam climbed up to near the top of the mountain that stood near their home. He came across the entrance to a big dark cave that he hadn't seen before, and he thought that, maybe, there would be some good dry wood inside. But, just as he put one foot inside, an ugly great monster came out of the darkness towards him.

Sam ran away as fast as he could and managed to climb a tree. Luckily, he had carried his drum with him up the mountain and he started beating it – boom, boom, boom…. The monster sat down at the foot of the tree, listening to the drum. Slowly the monster's eyes began to close and he fell into a deep sleep. Sam climbed down from the tree, slipped past the sleeping monster and ran home as fast as he could. He told his parents and his aunt about what had happened and they all went up the mountain to the cave to drive the monster away, his father holding his knife out in front of him. But the monster was a little cleverer than they thought. They peered into the darkness of the cave but could not see the ugly beast. Suddenly he appeared behind them and gobbled up Sam's parents and his aunt in three great gulps.

Sam managed to slip away while the monster was swallowing and climbed the same tree again; and again he began beating his drum – boom, boom, boom…. The monster sat down at the foot of the tree and, exactly as before, fell asleep. Sam picked up his father's knife that had been dropped by the cave and cut open the monster's stomach. His father, mother and his aunt all tumbled out and Sam's family strolled happily back home together.

Superstar

Vimbai Mucheriwa

Being a superstar
To have the glitz and the glamour
The fame and the fortune
It would be great wouldn't it?
I would be known all over
People would fight over a T-shirt
With my face on it
I would have money to burn
Buying things I wouldn't even use
That I would never need.

Being a superstar
I would have my own chauffeur
Taking me from place to place
I wouldn't have to lift a finger
I would have people to do all the work
I would blind everyone
With my sparkling rubies and diamonds
I would enchant them
With my perfume.

Being a superstar
Having friends wouldn't be a problem
If I wanted I could buy them
As many as I wanted
Who would say no to me
Because I'm a superstar.

Being a superstar
Truly I don't think it would be good for me
I am afraid of how I would turn out
Ending up forgetting where I came from
Being someone that I'm not
Forgetting who my real family is
No, being a superstar is not for me.

Courage My Love

Gary Vundhla

I now believe that everything comes to an end. I wept day and night wondering what the next day would bring forth and how I would defend myself from the beast, but my answer was always the tears that streamed down my cheeks.

Naturally Courage did not remember anything that happened that day, as it was her first day to take a breath in this cruel world, but, later, she was told everything that occurred. Her mother always told her that the day she was born happiness poured into the family. Courage remembered her saying, 'Before I gave birth to you, your father and I were expecting a baby girl and, guess what, our expectations were fulfilled.' Courage loved it when her father shared with her how he felt before she was born. He told her he had waited for hours outside the labour room. He even imitated the actions he made, walking back and forth. All her father could hear were the agonizing screams of his beloved wife.

Courage had finally arrived in the early morning of June at about 6.30 am. Her mother told her that when she held Courage in her arms there was an immediate bond between them. Courage did not have many memories of her childhood but what few she had were fond memories, memories that made her smile. She remembered when her mother and father would throw her into the air and catch her again. This was such fun and she almost believed she could fly, she even remembered singing the R. Kelly song, *I believe I can fly.*

Sometimes her parents would watch her playing on the lawn following the tiny insects that roamed on the surface with her eyes. Playing hide and seek was her favourite game. She was fond of hiding in the wardrobe until one day she fell asleep inside. Her parents were both sick with worry and after a long search they reported her missing to the police. Her father thought they should go out and search for her while they waited for the police. He opened the wardrobe to collect a jacket and saw her sleeping peacefully with a smile on her face. She seemed in a world of her own, calmly sleeping while her parents were frantic with worry. All these

13

events of her childhood happened without her being aware that a dark cloud was following her. Her world would soon change.

Long after it happened Courage could still hear the shrieking. The brakes screamed on the hot road and without warning, BOOM! The horrendous accident claimed her mother's life. Courage was left severely disabled. If she revisited the scene of the accident in her mind and concentrated very hard, she could see the tyre marks imprinted on the ground and her mother lying lifeless beside the car. Sometimes everything came flooding back to her and it was as if it was happening all over again. At times like this it was like she was watching a movie right there on the street, a movie she had seen too many times and knew by heart. It was as if the sun had set for the Courage she had been and had risen on a cloudy day for a completely different Courage. She was now a girl who depended on others for everything. All she could do for herself was to inhale and exhale. As she could no longer speak, she used a tablet for communication.

The death of her mother left a huge gap in the family that no one could fill. Her father was worried that his daughter was lonely and he thought it would be best to find a new wife so that his daughter would grow up surrounded by a mother's love. Little did he know that the black cloud that was hanging over them would grow yet darker. When Courage heard that her father was getting married again she was sad and thought that her father had never loved her mother or how could he forget her so soon. She didn't realise that her father was doing it out of love for her.

The truth was that, since the terrible day of the accident, her father loved her more than ever and treated her like a princess because she brought back memories of his dead wife. When Mr Sibanda got married again he did not know the kind of woman he was bringing into the family and the pain she would inflict on his own daughter.

The father was blinded by love and wanted to do his best for Courage. He was convinced that everything was going well in his family. Changes at work meant that he had to relocate and leave his family behind, but he did not see this as too great a problem because he thought that Courage was in caring hands. Unfortunately his new wife turned out to be a snake in the grass. When her father was around she would shower Courage with affection and convince him that she really loved the child. In reality her heart was as hard as a rock. The stepmother was mean and unfeeling and Courage thought that maybe she had a steel heart because she did not feel anyone else's pain. Courage was depressed and she no longer laughed or smiled the way she used to do. Her stepmother neglected her and would not bath her for weeks and gave her very little food. She told Courage she deserved to die because she was a burden.

Courage only found comfort around her father when he came home from work or when relatives came to visit. Courage felt that she shared her home with a beast. Even though her stepmother looked human on the outside, her soul was tainted with darkness. To everyone else she was kind, especially to her own daughter, Angelina. She told Courage that Angelina would inherit her father's money as someone crippled like Courage could never amount to anything. Courage's skin became grey from lack of care and attention, but Mr Sibanda still believed that he had found a good mother for his daughter because he did not see the real way his wife treated Courage.

Courage had many things she wanted to tell her father but she always failed, because when they were alone and he asked her how she was she could not tell him because her stepmother had removed her tablet with the excuse that it needed to be recharged. Mr Sibanda was fond of Angelina but Courage was the reason he woke up every day with renewed strength to face the challenges ahead.

Angelina loved her stepsister but, because of her mother, felt unable to show Courage affection. Courage became tired of all the pretence when her father was around, when the house would be filled with love and smiles. Then the beast transformed to an angel.

Courage's father had no idea about the reality of his daughter's life. He always paid her school fees but Courage did not attend school because her stepmother said she didn't deserve to learn. Mr Sibanda would boast to his colleagues that Courage was in good hands but his friends would say that all that glitters is not gold. He would then tell them that few women would take a disabled child with them everywhere they went. Little did he know that when they went to visit friends Courage was left alone in the car.

It is said that everything that is done in the darkness will be revealed in the light. Mr Sibanda had a dream and in it Courage told him that she was being treated badly. 'Dad, God gave me a voice so that I can use it only this once, please listen to me. I am not happy at home, the happiness you see there is pretence, please help me.' With these words she lost her voice again. Mr Sibanda was troubled by this dream and he sent his lawyer to survey the situation at home.

The lawyer visited the Sibanda household over a week. He didn't see anything that proved that Courage was being ill-treated. He applauded Mrs Sibanda and told her that, if they treated Courage well, they might be lucky to inherit the family business because everything would belong to

Courage. The lawyer's words encouraged the stepmother to plot against Couráge. When she heard that everything would be left to her stepdaughter upon her husband's death she knew that she must do what she ought to have done a long time ago. She must kill Courage!

Mrs Sibanda cooked Courage's favourite meal and put poison in it. Angelina was afraid and tried to plead on Courage's behalf. She tried to talk sense into her mother's head and said that instead of killing her they should love her so that she would agree to stay with them. Mrs Sibanda took no heed of her daughter's pleading.

Poor Courage died a peaceful and painless death. Her stepmother cried more than anyone. Angelina was shocked that her mother had achieved what she wanted and was still able to cry. Mr Sibanda was contacted to be told that Courage had died. He was heartbroken and depressed but because of his work commitments he was delayed and only arrived as the coffin was being lowered into the ground. He just stared and the coffin slowly but surely went down towards the dust. He could not believe that Courage was gone for good and he would never see her twinkling eyes and smile whenever he shouted 'Courage, I'm home.' He was very quiet and no one noticed his presence because everyone was lost in their own thoughts. Before anyone could stop him he shouted, 'Wait, wait.' The coffin was hovering just above the ground and everyone turned their heads towards him and labelled him a madman. He ordered the burial to stop because he wanted to see his daughter's face one last time. The coffin was raised and he looked at his daughter as if she was sleeping peacefully. She looked so beautiful as if she was about to wake up and say 'hi dad'.

Mr Sibanda said he wanted to know the cause of his daughter's death before he buried her. His wife told him that it was too late because she was afraid that she might be caught. Mr Sibanda stared at her in surprise but he continued to demand a post-mortem and a thorough investigation. The body was examined and it was found that she had been poisoned.

Mr Sibanda could not believe it. He couldn't think who would have poisoned his princess. Mrs Sibanda said they must have poisoned her at school. She didn't know that by saying that she had stepped on the tail of a sleeping snake. Mr Sibanda questioned the school authorities and was shocked when they told him that Courage never attended school. He did not understand because he had been sending money for school fees. When she was asked about this Mrs Sibanda started stammering and said they were lying.

He went back to the mortuary and asked the doctors about the poison and they told him it had been taken with mashed potatoes made with butter and milk. He knew this was Courage's favourite meal and he knew that no one except the family would know this. He was now very confused but still did not think it could be anyone in the family. That night he had a strange dream. In the dream Courage told him not to give up because he was about to catch the killer, the killer was in the house and he was the next target. He was troubled by his dream and asked his wife what Courage had eaten before she died. She told him and he went very quiet.

It just happened that the police were in the neighbourhood going about their errands and they came close to Mr Sibanda's house. Courage's death was haunting Mrs Sibanda and when she saw the police coming towards her she threw herself to the ground and said, 'I will confess, I will tell you everything I know.' The police were surprised and they asked her what she meant. She quickly realized she was about to send herself to jail so instead she told them that she could not kill her own child, she could not be that cruel. The police listened as she denied her evil deeds. Then she told them that the day the dish was cooked it was Angelina who was cooking and that maybe it was her, because she had always hated her stepsister. The policemen fell for the lie and accused Angelina and took her off to the police station. But Angelina had had enough and she quickly told them the whole story. The police were convinced by Angelina's story, she was released and the police went off to arrest her mother.

Mr Sibanda was pleased that the detective work had finally revealed the truth. He buried his daughter with the knowledge of what had really happened. He never married again and, being a loving man, he took good care of Angelina by giving her all the love and care she deserved.

I Will Never Cry

Alice Senda

Yes, I did not shed any tears
My mother and her wrinkled face
The sarcastic, scornful smile on her lips
The unkempt long grey hair
The sandpaper hands, which were a blessing.

Yes, she spoke eloquently of the life she lived
How she was and how we were
How she built a clay pot with mud
How she thatched her kitchen roof
How she polished her floor with cow dung.

Yes, I did not shed a tear
How she looked after our father, her husband
How she took good care of us and how we grew
Everything she ever did for her family
I could not cry for even a single day.

Yes, the wisdom she gave me
Washing, cooking and cleaning
She taught me to cook traditional foods
Though her dreams of freedom and happiness
Had become my song, my love
I had already inherited her love
Yes she is gone, gone for good
But I could not cry for her.

I could not cry, but will forever miss her works
My mother's dead life still lives in me and in my daughter
I am the daughter of my mother and the mother of my daughter
My mother became the fruit of my life
But I will never cry for her.

Where is My Mother?

Anesu Zhira

In 1998 I lived in Chibi with my grandmother. They say I was a clever boy but that I cried a lot because I was lonely. One day, when I was four years old, I went to Victoria Falls with my mother and sister to join my father. When I saw the bus that was going to take us there I was frightened because I had stayed for such a long time in the village with no cars, no buses and no motorbikes.

I liked playing with my older sister, but one day she woke up in the morning and started putting on a uniform. I asked my mother why she was wearing a uniform and I was told she was going to school.

'What about me?' I cried.

'You're still a baby,' my mother replied.

'Me, me, me, I am not a baby and I need to go to school with my sister,' I shouted.

I started washing myself so that I could go to school, but she said. 'You are a good boy but you do not have a uniform and if you don't have a uniform they will not accept you at school.'

I cried and cried and my mother said, 'Sorry baby, but you will be able to go to school soon.'

When my sister came back home from her first day at school and greeted me I ignored her, 'Why should I be happy to see you when you left me at home?'

Mother told my father that I really wanted to go to school, but he said I was just a young boy. When I asked him why my sister was going if I couldn't, he got angry and I started to feel frightened.

When I was six years old my mother told me that I was going to school the next day. But, of course, I didn't want to go to school any more. I hated the idea of going to school because up until then I had spent my time playing with my friends. I had to go, but, at first, I felt lost and I started to cry for my mother. She came to comfort me, and I started to understand and to like school.

Soon I was doing well at school, passing all my subjects. Then we lost my father. My mother and sister cried all the time. I was ten years old. My mother went to work in Bulawayo, leaving me, and my sister, in Victoria Falls to stay with an uncle. We never saw or heard from her again. My uncle is a fierce man and he often beats me for reasons I don't understand. His wife then started to beat me as well, so my life has become a misery.

A year later, I often dream about the happy life I used to have with my father and mother. My sister tries to comfort me, telling me not to give up. But I still often cry out, 'Where is my mother?'

Journey to the Desert

Thandazani Khoza

Life in the Garden of Eden was good. Animals, plants, trees and God communicated well and with understanding. Plants fed animals and animals fertilized the soil.

As I sat down, an orphan who has just finished writing Grade 7 exams, I wished that those old days would come back into being. If you are an orphan, planning for your future is a joke. You do not have a Garden of Eden where you are allowed to dream and where dreams come true, where you have parents as role models, where you go for days without shedding tears. Dreaming of an earthly Garden of Eden, a place where you can live happily ever after, is like rain in the desert.

Most orphans do not have a permanent place to live. You are like a nomad. You keep moving from place to place. Not in search of greener pastures but looking for people who are willing to accommodate you. Preparing for my first national exams was like heaven on earth. It kept me busy. Appreciation and encouragement from my teacher made me feel like a human being. Now it is all over and, when relatives visit, all the household chores are mine. No time to sit and relax. 'How were the exams?' is a common question. 'Easy,' I reply. Instead of getting some form of affection a bucket-full of negative comments is poured on me. At times I try to change the answer to, 'They were difficult'. Worse. 'You must look for a job as a maid for you are a good for nothing,' they will say.

I go back through my exercise books, which have a lot of encouraging comments. Teachers adopt, love and push a class forward. Once your time is over with a particular teacher, it is over. At times I try to communicate directly with God. I try and listen hard, hoping to hear words from my dear dead parents.

I try hard to remember my dreams, hoping to get affection from my parents, but it is too late. All I remember vividly is, 'Be good my daughter, AIDS is real and it kills.' These are the words that I treasure from my mother before they both left this world for a world I do not want to imagine. Left, leaving me alone, no brother, no sister.

My parents were very unfortunate; the disease attacked them both at the same time. My mother's parents blamed my father for bringing the disease; they wanted to take my mother back to their home but she refused. My mother had promised my father, till death do us part. Indeed death did separate them, for my mother was buried in her home area while my father died in town. So that was it, poor me left all by myself. I was still too young then to understand what was going on. At first it was a relief for I was the one who had been taking care of the invalids. Being around sick people in pain is not easy. So being around healthy people cooking and enjoying food made me feel better. People all around me feeling sorry for me. This gave me hope that these were caring people, I thought they were going to put their resources together for my upkeep.

Traditionally meetings are held at that time to plan the family's future. But I soon realized that for me this was the beginning of a long journey from Egypt to the desert, not Canaan as I hoped.

Life Ain't Treating Me So Well

Chipo Mazodze

Life is like an adventure
It has its ups and downs
Everything I thought I knew has gone
Because life ain't treating me so well.

I look outside the window at the pouring rain
Tears are shifting down my cheeks
The wind blows; I feel the cold inside the house
Because life ain't treating me so well.

I go to bed, try to sleep but I can't
I toss and turn but sleep eludes me
I am awake all night
Because life ain't treating me so well

I try to eat but I can't
The food won't go down my throat
I try to speak but no one hears me
I cry but no one is there to comfort me
Because life ain't treating me so good.

I go out of the house to get fresh air
But when I walk in the streets
I feel everyone pointing at me
'Look at her, she has no shoes'
Because life ain't treating me so well.

Her Own Two Feet

Sarah Mareni

John was born in the village of Kangaru. He was the only one of his colour in the whole area as he had a mixed heritage, with a black father and a white mother. His mother died when he was very young and he lived with his father in Kangaru until he was sixteen. His father then went to work in South Africa and he had to stand on his own two feet. When John was still sixteen he met a lovely girl of his own age. Their sweet sixteen romance resulted in the couple having a child within a short time.

John, now a father himself, had not completed his education, so he was unable to find a qualified job. He became a builder as he knew a little about the building trade and was able to do some piece-work to support his new family. The young mother, Farai, was a full-time home worker. Their child, Chipo, looked like her grandmother from her father's side, just as her father did. Even as a small child she only had eyes for her father, rarely exchanging words with anyone else. And John wanted to spend all his time with Chipo. As soon as she was four years old, John took the child wherever he went and she never spent any time with her mother to talk mother/daughter talk. Sadly, it was as if, with the appearance of the child, the love of the parents for each other vanished.

John had not paid lobola to Farai's family so there were constant fights between the couple. Despite being tempted Farai did not return to live with her family. Then, out of the blue and for an inexplicable reason, one beautiful day John decided he should marry his wife properly. He went to visit her family and they were excited and happy that he had come to pay the lobola. This was the first time that Chipo had spent any time alone with her mother as her father had left the two together. Before he left on his journey to visit his wife's family John expressed his love for his wife, the first time for many years. Sadly his wife had become ill by this time, which also made life for the young family difficult.

On his way back from visiting his wife's family, John bought a present for Farai. In the box that held the present he put a letter that he had written to her. The letter read, 'To my beloved wife, I love you so much.

Forgive me all the wrong things I did to you over the years. I love you, my wife, and I need you.' He was so excited that the long journey became short for him. But his happiness was short-lived because on the way home he was involved in a bus accident.

This was the day Chipo had to really grow up, even though she was still only twelve years old, as, sadly, her father died from his injuries. John's death resulted in Farai's condition deteriorating and she became very ill. So Chipo still didn't get to spend time with her mother, as she was now too ill. The only time Chipo had really spent time alone with her mother was when her father left them to go to pay the lobola.

Farai was soon admitted to hospital where she stayed for two months before she died. Chipo was devastated to be left alone after losing both her parents in so short a time. She would now have to learn to stand on her own two feet.

Be Thankful For What You Have

Vimbai Mucheriwa

Be thankful for what you have
Do not let your heart fool you
Into wanting something that you cannot have
Do not let your eyes fool you
Into wanting something you don't need
And do not let your mind fool you
Into thinking you want something that you do not.

Be thankful for what you have
What you have might not be as attractive
What you have might not taste as good
What you have won't seem like much
But I know what you have is as good as gold
So treat it as such.

Be thankful for what you have
What you have is what you need
If you can survive with what you have
Why want something different?
If you can live life as it is
Why wish for something different?

Be thankful for what you have
To want something is one thing
To need something is another
If you have what you need
Then what you want doesn't matter
If you do or don't have it
What you need is what matters most.

How to Love

Primrose Ndlovu

'Doctor, you might have made a mistake, please go and check again,' pleads Miss Jiyane with tears streaming down her cheeks. How could this happen was the question on her mind. All the men she had slept with looked healthy and none of them had shown signs of being HIV positive. She rested on the chair as her mind drifted to a faraway place.

Jasmine Jiyane had grown up living on the streets and she never knew the meaning of family and belonging. Her family were the kids on the street and some of the kind people who sometimes gave her food. One night a kind lady drove up to her as she was looking for supper in a bin. She spoke to her in a kind calm voice and the fear in Jasmine disappeared. The lady gave her food and bid her good night. The visits continued and Jasmine would even go for rides in the lady's luxurious car.

One day the kind lady came but did not bring any food. Jasmine was surprised as she had got used to being spoilt, she would eat chicken and rice while the other street kids were fighting for leftover bones in the bins. The lady said she had come to take care of her as if she was her own daughter. Jasmine was as happy as a pig in muck. She did not even say goodbye to her friends who had been her family for the past ten years. She imagined how her life would be and she saw herself transforming from zero (street kid) to hero (millionaire).

The kind lady introduced herself as Mrs Phiri and explained to Jasmine that she was a widow with no children. She told Jasmine that she would adopt her. For the first few months everything ran smoothly. Jasmine was showered with love and treated like a princess. She was sent to school and she felt on top of the world. There was only one thing she didn't understand and that was why different men came to the house each evening and then left early in the morning.

Jasmine showed a lot of interest in her school work and her grades were excellent. She really wanted to make Mrs Phiri happy. After a year suddenly everything changed. Mrs Phiri no longer smiled and one night she told Jasmine she was old enough to look after herself and that she must drop out of school. Jasmine began to protest but Mrs Phiri just told her that the next day she was not going to school but she would be joining the 'ladies' club'.

Jasmine was hurt and she could not believe that the person she had called mother was turning her back on her. The young girl had no choice but to join the ladies club. She became a prostitute and a drug addict. She would sleep with different rich men without protection. Suddenly everything was about money and drugs. Mrs Phiri was very happy, she would bring men to the house and all of them wanted to sleep with Jasmine.

Doctor Khuphe disturbed Jasmine's thoughts to tell her that she was not only HIV positive but also pregnant. As she slowly but surely digested these words her life looked bleak. She wanted the best for her unborn child. She did not want her to go along the same humiliating path as her. She wanted her daughter to live her own dream of becoming rich but most of all she wanted her daughter to be loved and not to be shy of showcasing her parents to her friends.

She knew that all these wishes were impossible. She was a prostitute who had no idea who the father of the child was. She was a drug addict and where would she get the money for her child's education. She thought of abortion but the thought of killing a human being made her shudder. She thought of adoption but the way she had turned out she was too afraid of the way her daughter might be treated. Jasmine had never been shown true love. Everyone who said they loved her had done so for their own benefit.

She left the hospital a changed woman, with a new vision and a goal in life. She ran away from Mrs Phiri and looked for work as a housemaid. She wanted to show Mrs Phiri and the other members of the ladies club how to love through your child. A kind old couple gave her work and a place to stay. With the first month's salary she went to a rehabilitation centre so that she could stop her addiction.

The 25th December 1985 was a day that Jasmine would never forget. It was a day that brought joy and happiness into her life. When everyone was celebrating the birth of Christ, Jasmine was celebrating the birth of Innocencia, her innocent child who would have to suffer the consequences of her mother's life style. Innocencia was HIV positive from birth but she grew up surrounded by love. She went to the best schools that her mother could afford and she was taught the dangers of drugs and prostitution. Finally Jasmine knew she would have to tell Innocencia her status. She told her that she was HIV positive and explained that the reason the other women in the community never wanted to see Jasmine talking to their husbands was because she used to be a prostitute. Jasmine told her daughter about the rough path she had travelled and the hardships she had endured. Mother and daughter embraced with tears streaming down their cheeks. Innocencia now understood why the other children did not want to play with her and why she and her mother were outcasts.

Whoever said the sky is the limit said so because she failed to go beyond it, but Innocencia proved the saying wrong. She fulfilled her mother's wishes of becoming a successful businesswoman. She is now happily married and living positively with her condition. Her mother, sadly, is dead, but Innocencia always remembers the three most important things she learnt from her mother: how to love, how to forgive, and never to give up in life, but the greatest of these three was how to love!

What Next?

Elisha Gumbo

There once was a boy of fifteen. Born in March 1998 at Kadoma General Hospital, he lived with his parents and young brother. Growing up he was able bodied. He started to go to school in 2003 and from the zero grade he progressed to the 7th grade.

Unfortunately, on 14th February 2011, when he was in Grade 7 something terrible happened to this boy. He was walking back from school as he had done every day of his school life, but this time as he walked along the path, which was mainly used by pedestrians, he did not know that there was an electric cable on the ground. As he walked along the path he stepped on it and was electrocuted.

Later the boy heard that he had been helped by people who were passing by and who found him collapsed on the ground. He woke up to find himself in hospital, critically ill. When he looked at himself he thought it was a dream or rather a nightmare, but it was reality. He was put on medication that made him feel drowsy and resulted in him sleeping for three days. When he woke up he saw his family crying, saying 'Why us, oh Lord, why us?' and he started to cry as well.

His hands and arms had been amputated by doctors in the hospital and, when his wounds were cleaned, he would cry for hours in pain. He stayed in the hospital for nearly five months and then he was discharged, but he was still not yet physically strong. Everything in his life seemed upside down because he could not do many of the things that he used to do on his own. He could not wash himself, feed himself, put on clothes by himself, write for himself or even take himself to the toilet. His mother cried each and every day and she lost hope for her son. His face and other parts of his body were covered with scars that itched. Looking at himself in the mirror was like a nightmare and he would cry and cry until his head started to ache.

July came and went and he was still not physically strong and he avoided people most of the time. August and September passed and October came, the month of his final primary exams. He said to himself 'I will write the exams', but the question arose as to how he would be able to write. The school's head assured him that some of the teachers would write down the answers as he gave them. The problem remained that he had missed so much schooling that he might not know the answers. However, he was encouraged by his family, who told him that with God everything is possible. With their support he sat the examinations. October and November passed and it was December when the results came out. The boy went to collect them and found himself amongst those who had passed. He was very happy that day.

Afterwards he asked himself, 'What next?' He started to cry when he wondered what he would do. While he was crying a person from King George VI School for the Disabled called and said he should come to the school because of the facilities there that would help him to learn to do things on his own. He was really relieved.

The boy is still finding everything difficult in life but he knows that one day he will make it, if he keeps on fighting hard. Nothing will dampen his spirit.

I am what I am

Michelle Mabaleka

I am what I am
Because I know where I come from
Everyone asks where I come from
And I answer them with confidence.

Some say I am black, white, yellow
But I am what I am.
This world is full of different people
But every one of them knows their ancestors
What you are is the pride in your heart.

Some might say disability is inability
I am proud to say that I am what I am
I was created to live.
Every person was created in God's image
Yet no one knows how God looks.
I am assured of being the right image
As is everyone, I am what I am!

So I say to each and everyone
Be proud of who you are
Forget every voice that separates you
From being your voice.
I am what I am!

A Journey to Botswana

Paidashe Yolanda Tekede

One morning I was busy cleaning the house when my mum surprised me when she told me that my father, who was working in Botswana, wanted to see us. My mum's news came as a shock because he had never asked us to visit him there before. I went to bathe so fast as I so looked forward to seeing my father, and to see another country. After I had bathed and got dressed I packed some clothes into my little bag. My mother, my brother and I then went to catch the bus. We got on the bus, the engine started and we were off, driving and driving on the way to Botswana, but first to Bulawayo.

Through the window I saw so many different trees, watched the baboons sitting by the side of the road and the men selling oranges and sweets and other things. I looked up at the sky and then turned my face to my mother. She smiled at me. I smiled too and then turned to look at my brother, but he was fast asleep.

The bus stopped in the city of Bulawayo and the driver asked if anyone wanted to go to the toilet. Of course we took the chance to go and then my mother and I bought some fruit and pizza. I shook my brother awake him so he could also go to the toilet. After thirty minutes the driver started up the engine, so we got back into our seats on the bus and started to eat. I took the pizza and my mother started to laugh because she knew I was greedy like a pig. Now with a full stomach, I looked out of the window and saw it was like a mirror.

I saw my face in the window and asked my mother, 'Am I beautiful?'

'Of course you look beautiful' she said. I smiled and turned back to the window and watched the different types of tree and all the different animals. It was a long, long way to travel. After a while my eyes grew tired and I dozed off. We travelled and travelled on the road, all the way to the border post at Plumtree. The bus stopped and we took out our passports to show to the immigration officials. Then we travelled for another few kilometres across into Botswana, where we had to show our passports again.

My mother and my young brother were happy because the journey was safe, even if it was a long way.

'Is it further than to travel from Bulawayo to Harare,' I asked my mother and she answered that of course it is.

After the border, we travelled again for what seemed hours until we finally reached Francistown in Botswana. I had dropped off to sleep and my mother shook me awake and showed me the town. I smiled at my mother and asked if we would stop here. My mother whispered no and I sighed. 'Your father lives in Maun, which is much further.' I sighed again and I looked out of the window and saw people walking by so I waved at them. We got off the bus to buy some more food and then got back on to the bus to continue the journey.

In the evening people on the bus started to sing songs praising the Lord, while others chatted amongst themselves. It was getting cold so we put on our jerseys. I wriggled in my seat as I could not be patient any longer and I complained to my mother. I said it was too far to travel but my mother and brother both laughed at me. After seven hours she shook me from sleep and, smiling, told me the journey was over and we had finally arrived. I sat up and saw the town of Maun. It is in a very beautiful area.

My father was waiting for us and I got out of the bus and I ran to him. My brother and I gave him a big hug and my mother looked happy. My father took our things to his car and we laughed and chatted. We had lots of fun on the way to his home. I was so pleased to see him. It was worth the long journey.

How Life Can Be

Vimbai Mucheriwa

Sometimes people have the unkindness of ravens; I'm talking about stabbing a person in the back, kicking a person when he's down for no reason at all. That is what happened to my father. My father worked for a company for thirty years, putting all his effort, his heart and his utmost concentration into the business that would later forget him. Oh my poor father, whose heart glowed like a candle, but now it is pitch black because of the people who blew it out, who took away his trust.

When my father joined the company he was a dark horse and no one knew what to expect. They thought he had nothing exceptional to offer but when he sat down and was given transactions, cashbooks and journals, he knew exactly what to do with them. God had blessed him; it was as if he understood accounts from the first moment he could utter the words 'da da'. Now my father considers this gift was actually a curse.

Dad loved doing his job. He didn't feel reluctant about getting up for work when he woke up in the morning because he loved his work. If you have a gift, why not share it with the world? At the beginning of the day he would sit at his desk with a pile of paper work stacked in front of him and by the end of the day he would have finished everything. The company never even thanked him. Never gave him any form of recognition for the good work or congratulated him for a job well done. They just expected more from him and when he gave them more, they wanted even more. It was because of his good management that they were able to open restaurants and bars. Because of him they were able to make even more revenue. Then what did they do? They kicked him into the gutter, threw him away like used tissue paper. How did they do this? They lied!

He did not work so hard for extra money on top of his pay. He never asked them to buy him a new house, a new car. He bought a car from his own savings and those who were envious became even more so. They started asking questions about where he had come by the money. They had their own cars, bigger cars than he drove, but they still had the nerve to ask him where he got his car. They talked about him just because he was trying

35

his best to be someone in the world. But they could not live with that; they wanted him to remain a little 'Oliver Twist', begging for more.

My father is a quiet man. He said nothing. He would sit on the couch and read his novels and feel at peace with himself. This made him feel better inside. What happened to him was so unfair but we couldn't do anything about it. He had to go through it alone but we were always there to console him. The company then showed their true colours. They started by not paying him at all. My mother wanted to go to the office and plead with the bosses but my father wouldn't let her. He said that even though he was not getting paid he would always have a plan to bring food to the table and he meant what he said.

As if not getting paid wasn't enough, they lied and accused him of stealing money. That was the last straw. Getting no recognition for the good job he did was one thing, but being blamed for something that you know in your heart is not true, that was too much. Seeing all those that you called friends siding with the enemy really tore my father's spirit apart. These people had sold him down the river.

My father then started drinking a lot, trying to drown his pain, reading novels wasn't working anymore. I didn't like the fact that he was drinking but when he wasn't drinking he was shouting about how cruel the world can be. I felt sorry for him as he lay there drunk and sleepy. We understood exactly what he was going through.

Eventually he left the job he had loved for so long. After what they did to him he had no choice, he just couldn't take it anymore. The case was taken to court and it turned out that God hadn't completely forgotten him as there was no evidence against him, only rumours.

I asked him if he would ever go back if they were to apologise. He said he would never go back as his heart would not let him. The people from the company had shown him such hate he would never be able to work among them again.

He now waits for what rightfully belongs to him. Now he does what he can to keep going. I don't ask him too many questions, I'm afraid to. So yes, people can be that heartless. It's funny how life can be.

Neglected but Happy

Thandazani Khoza

Here I am sitting alone
Under the baobab tree as usual,
I sit here all day long
In my wheelchair.
No one bothers to chat
I sit here with the ants biting
But no one seems to notice.

Other children laugh at me
Kick me or spit on me
And no one cares
Not even my brothers and sisters.

No one speaks to me
Or even looks at me
They all think I am a curse.

I sit here all day long
And everyone forgets me
Do they even wonder
If I am hungry or thirsty?

Every morning my family
Prepare their own food
They forget about me
But I do not care.

Although the ants may bite
The other children laugh
And point fingers at me
I do not mind.

I am happy the way I am
And as pleased as punch
For being alive
And a part of this world
And I know that God
Has a reason for me to live.

What Words Cannot Describe

Abigail Ncube

Have you ever been in pain? I mean physical pain, pain you cannot describe. Maybe talk to mothers about labour pains. I am yet to meet a mother who can clearly describe labour pain. I gathered this information as we were doing our guidance and counselling lessons.

On this particular day, three of my teachers were talking about teenage pregnancy. They each took turns to describe their experiences but all I gathered was – it's painful. How? All you could see were queer expressions on their faces and shaking of heads from side to side. Then why do people keep on having babies?

With questions rushing through my mind I went home. I got home and my favourite aunt had paid a visit. As per tradition I share my bedroom with female visitors. Good arrangement, for it was going to give me time to get a better description of labour pain. For at that point I was not sure whether to go to a convent, become a nun and skip the baby business, or be brave about it like other women.

After supper we had our usual prayers and I closed our bedroom door ready to start a new session with my aunt. As if God had whispered something in her ears, my aunt started talking about friendship, good and bad friends, feelings towards the opposite sex – you know how boring that can be! They will go on and on! As I listened attentively, waiting for my chance to ask, I remembered that my aunt had had three miscarriages. After the fourth pregnancy she had a son, Munyaradzi. Now I wasn't sure whether to ask, or how to ask without hurting her feelings. She went on with her talk and finally she talked about the pain. She talked of the kind of pain that I had never imagined, much worse than the pain my teachers had failed to describe. It was the pain of losing her three babies. To make matters worse, the pain of giving birth to an HIV positive baby.

It's like she had found an empty pit where to empty her bucket full of sorrows. I was the pit where all the pain was poured. I tried to hold back my tears but I could not. I held her hand and gave her the ear she so longed for.

Munyaradzi was not well, he was not responding to the ARVs. My aunt wanted to ask for money from my father to take him to specialists. I rubbed her hand hard trying to understand. My aunt looked well and happy, a jovial woman. 'Why, Lord'? I asked. 'Look before you jump' was the advice she gave me. I do not know how but I lost track of what she was saying and I fell asleep.

Next morning we woke up happy and I prepared to go to school. It was as if that talk had evaporated from my brain. I got to school and was well until break time. The three teachers were together laughing, at what I did not know. I looked at them and paused. The talk of the previous night became vivid and fresh. Poor ladies, there is no adjective or adverb that can describe pain. With tears in my eyes I took a walk to the playground.

The Wise Boy

Tsitsi Marenga

Once upon a time there was a boy named Ruzvimbo. He knew nothing but village life. He had a family; among other family members Ruzvimbo had three brothers, Rangarai, the eldest, followed by Samson, then Tinoda the last-born.

They lived in Buera village. The other village boys did not get on with Ruzvimbo because he only talked about herding cattle. Apart from Tinoda who loved him, his two other brothers were like the other village boys in not liking him. One day his uncle came and took Ruzvimbo to Harare, where he was to attend school.

Unfortunately, Ruzvimbo did not take his schoolwork seriously. This disappointed his uncle; he had expected more effort from him. His uncle took Ruzvimbo back to the village, which upset Ruzvimbo's parents. The boy saw the error of his ways and apologised for his behaviour.

After Ruzvimbo spent two weeks at home in the village, his uncle returned to collect him. Ruzvimbo made a promise to his parents that this time he would take his studies seriously. The young man returned to Harare where he studied at Kutonga Primary School. His parents were now happy. His brothers were so unhappy with Ruzvimbo being the one chosen by their uncle to be taken away and educated that they planned to poison him.

Rangarai and Samson plotted against Ruzvimbo but had not taken into account that Tinoda, who knew of their plans, was kind, and loved Ruzvimbo. When Ruzvimbo came back to the village to visit his family his two brothers pretended to be happy, hiding their real feelings from their brother. Fortunately their plan to poison their brother failed because Tinoda had spilt the beans to Ruzvimbo.

Ruzvimbo had grown up a lot while he was in the town studying and decided not to upset his parents by telling them of his brothers' plan to harm him. He acted as if nothing was wrong. Rangarai and Samson did not go ahead with their plan to poison their young brother on that visit, as Ruzvimbo was so careful.

Time went on and, on Ruzvimbo's next visit home, Rangarai and Samson decided that this time they would really try to poison him and keep their plan a secret from Tinoda. They bought biscuits, which they poisoned, but fortunately Ruzvimbo was a boy of wisdom and he refused to take the biscuits. Rangarai and Samson became angry and threatened Ruzvimbo, which Tinoda overheard. Tinoda immediately reported the matter to his father and mother. His parents were naturally shocked and the father ran immediately to where the boys were sitting.

Ruzvimbo was not there so was unable to confirm what Tinoda had told the parents, so the boys' father thought at first that his youngest son was lying and told him so. Tinoda started to cry and it was at that moment that Ruzvimbo returned.

'What is wrong?' Ruzvimbo asked Tinoda. When his brother explained what had happened, Ruzvimbo was able to tell his father that it was all true. At this the father spoke to the brothers who were accused of plotting to kill Ruzvimbo. The boys admitted what they had been plotting and apologized to Ruzvimbo. Their apology was accepted and the boys made up and from then on they lived together happily as a family.

Stepmother

Oleander Payarira

Her smile brightens my day,
The twinkle of her eye
Is like a twinkling star,
Her voice sounds like music to my ears.

Her heart is made of gold,
For she is a loving person,
Her cleanliness, orderliness, culinary skills,
All I love and admire.

A heroine, she is to me,
Her love for me is unconditional,
It is above human understanding.
Stepmother! Yes,
She is a step above ordinary mothers.

My dreams, she knows,
My weaknesses, she understands,
My strengths, she supports,
She is like the mother I've never had.

An amazon, she is,
She helps me in tough situations,
She is as wise as old Solomon,
That is why she advises me.

God, immaculate Father,
Thank you for this wonderful being,
Words cannot express my gratitude,
I wake up and sleep with a song in my heart,
This is all because of her.

Lord, bless her with eternal life, grace and joy,
Bless her, and fulfil her dreams,
Bless her worldly and heavenly riches,
For such beings can only be sheltered,
In the glory of Your palace.

Give her health,
May all be flourishing,
Find no comfort in this marvellous temple,
Like Dorcas in the bible,
Be blessed.

The Way Life Is

Ocean Maidza

Life is a journey, a process where one comes across good and tough times. In the beginning I knew nothing about how it felt to be an orphan. Now I can tell you that it feels like being lost in the middle of nowhere, left in the middle of the ocean.

This is a story with no beginning and no ending. It was on one of those days when I wasn't in school because my mother was suffering from cancer. My father, who I had never known, and my relatives turned their backs on me. I remember that day when I was sitting next to her, watching her cough up blood. I saw how thin she was, to the extent that none of her clothes fitted her anymore. There was little I could do, except to look at her and wait for the Creator to do His will.

Even then I woke up every morning looking forward to a brighter day. On that day I remember feeding my mother and everything that she ate came back out the same way. After this I did the household chores and for some reason the hairs on the back of my neck stood on end. I felt fear and I thought of my mother and I rushed to the single bed where she was lying. As I reached her everything seemed to stop, even the birds seem to stop singing their sweet melodies. The only thing I heard was the last groan of my mother and then she was gone. I fell down on my knees and screamed and asked the Lord how he could do such a terrible thing to me.

I did not know how I was going to tell my one and only sister, Lisa. She knew nothing about death and here we were left all alone to face the rough, unpredictable road. When Lisa came back from school, I told her and she wept like never before. I tried to comfort her but it was like beating her and the tears continued to flow.

With the help of neighbours we managed to bury my mother. What took me by surprise was that all my mother's relatives showed up for the funeral, when they had previously refused to help, even to buy medication. I could not get over the fact that she had passed away, but with time I began to accept it.

Now my main responsibility was to take good care of Lisa. Unfortunately things did not go the way I thought they would. Lisa was taken away from me along with every single thing that had belonged to my mother. At last I realized why they had all attended the funeral. Day and night there was quarrelling in the house about who was going to take this and who was going to take that. The most painful thing was they left nothing but the building itself and in barely a week people came to view even that. It seemed that even the last thing that I had thought I would be left with was being sold.

I live on the streets now and I have no blankets, my tattered clothes are my only source of warmth. I have not seen my beloved sister in a very long while. I hope that wherever she is that someone is taking good care of her. Indeed life is never a sweet song.

Cries of a Caregiver

Tanatswa Gwetsai

School days are the best. Our teacher asked us to design a timetable to follow now that we had finished our Grade seven exams. An argument arose. The majority wanted us to start at 10 am but my friend Abigail and I wanted to start at 8. My friend is a boarder and she would be alone at the hostel if we started later. My situation is different because my aunt who looks after me is not well. She depends on me. Whenever I get home she is relieved, as I take over the cooking, washing, cleaning the yard and bathing her two toddlers.

I am grateful, at least she is kind enough to have taken me in. I do not know anything about my father, and my mother left in 2008 for South Africa to look for a job. My aunt and my mother are good friends. My mother sends groceries, money and clothes, but she doesn't communicate with me. I last saw her when I was only six years old. She sends photos through Whatsapp but whenever she calls she only talks to my aunt. I will hear my aunt saying, 'She is well, doing fine.' My mother doesn't have the necessary papers so she can't pay us a visit.

When other people come to visit they bring fruit for my sick aunt and comfort her. They praise my aunt for training me to be a real woman. She replies, saying, 'She is hard working and thorough, I have trained her well.' It is my duty to remind her of the times to take her tablets. When she messes up, it's my duty to clean. Her neighbours praise my aunt for training me so well. She wakes me up in the middle of the night whenever she needs anything. She is not bedridden but she feels that she should rest whenever I am around. I am not allowed to play with my friends. Even if I could, I have so many duties that I do not have spare time to relax.

But the million dollar question is, who needs more love, care, affection and comfort – the affected or the infected!

The Bad Boy

Calvin Mwinde

I am that bad boy
Who everybody calls bad.
I am the baddest of the bad
But don't get me wrong
I am a lover not a fighter.
I make people make up
I don't make people break up.
But at least get this straight
I am the baddest of the bad.

I am that bad boy
Who dresses all in black
You can just call me a black man.
No, I am not a super-hero
But to other people I am a hero.
I don't care if people hate me
As long as my family loves me.

I am the bad boy.
I eat wherever I want,
I sleep wherever I want,
I drink wherever I want,
I party wherever I want.
I say I am a bad boy
Because that's what people say.

I am the bad boy
Every boy wants to be me.
All those who hate me, I'm sorry
But I will never change to somebody
You want me to be.

I don't care what people say about me
As long as my family loves me
Then all's good.

I am the bad boy
But at school I am not.
Yes, I know, I know
I am the baddest of the bad.
If you have teachers like mine
You would understand that
Education is the future
And knowledge is power.

I am the baddest of the bad.
Now don't get me wrong.
I can say whatever I want
I can do whatever I want
But without education
I can never be whatever I want,
But I will always be that bad boy.

Mary and Thandiwe's Story

Anonymous

My name is Mary and with me is my little sister Thandiwe. I think I am 17 years old and Thandiwe 13. I am not sure about our ages because we have lived alone for a long time. I am HIV positive and pregnant. I don't know if Thandiwe has the virus because she hasn't been tested yet.

This is my story.

My early memories are from living in Makokoba. This is a poor area of Bulawayo. I lived with my mother and father and we were okay. Then my father died when I was about six years old. I don't remember him very well; my little sister doesn't remember him at all. After my father died my mother needed to find work. She searched for jobs in Bulawayo but couldn't find anything. She heard from others that she could get work in South Africa. She left us in our house with some food and told us to talk to our neighbour if we needed help. She went to South Africa and did find work. She sent some money and then came back and stayed with us for a couple of weeks. The third time she went away we never heard from her again and no money was ever sent. We think she must have died because she would never have left us like this.

We ran out of food. Someone came to the house and told us we couldn't live there anymore. I am not sure who they were but we had to leave. We went to find my grandmother, my mother's mother. We found her after a few days but she didn't want us. We stayed with her for a while but I had to work very hard every day. My little sister was too young to work so she was beaten almost every day. It was a very unhappy place, so we ran away.

We lived on the streets. I tried to find work but couldn't find anything. We would stand on street corners and beg, but there were many beggars in the area and we never got very much. When I was standing on the street one day a man came and took me in his car. He offered me money for sex. I didn't want to but I had no other way to make money. I don't know how old I was the first time; I was probably 13 or 14. This became my life.

Sometimes I got paid, sometimes I got food and sometimes I was beaten up and dropped off in a different part of the city. But I had enough to feed my sister and me. Then I became pregnant, and none of the men wanted me anymore.

I tried to find work again and finally got a job as a domestic worker. I had to start work at six in the morning and work until the family went to bed. I had a small room to stay in. I asked if Thandiwe could stay with me but they said no, they didn't want another mouth to feed. My sister had been alone on the street for several weeks. I stole some clothes from my employer to try and sell so I could get money for food for my sister. I was caught and charged with theft. I went before a magistrate and admitted what I had done. The magistrate decided not to send me to jail. He tried to send me to a residential school where they would teach me a trade. But they wouldn't take me because I was pregnant.

The social worker I was assigned said he knew a man who took care of orphans and had a house where I might be able to stay. He called him and the Pastor came to pick me up. The Pastor did the paper work to take me in. He also said he would help find Thandiwe. That evening we went searching for her. We found that she was living in a house in Mzilikazi. She was working as a servant but she wasn't being paid, she was just getting food. She wasn't there when we arrived so we couldn't take her with us. The place she was living had a number of men living there. I was worried that they were hiding her. We kept searching for her and found her in the market later that night.

We are now both living with the Pastor's big family: he and his wife, seventeen orphaned girls and ten orphaned boys. Thandiwe and I are very happy to be here. For the first time since my mother left we feel that someone cares about us.

Lies

Gaudencia Rutize

I want to tell you a story. When I was young I could hear everything people were saying. I went to school with my friend as I was learning with other pupils who could hear. At that time my mother was working in Gweru and, one day, she came to collect me from the village as she had heard I was not well. I was so sick that I could not eat anything or do any work to help at home. I do not know what was wrong with me or what kind of a disease I had, I only know that I was always throwing up and my stomach was really painful. My mother rushed me to hospital, where I had to use an oxygen tank to breathe. She thought I was going to die because I could only breathe through the oxygen tank for three whole days. I don't remember anything of that time. Then, when I did wake up, I remember opening my eyes seeing my mother smiling down at me. Then I heard a very loud sound. My mother was calling me but I couldn't hear her properly. Throughout the next few days I could sometimes hear my mother's voice but it seemed to be from very far away although I could see her by my side. I cried and cried all the time. I also found it very difficult to stand up.

After two weeks I went to the rural areas in a scotch cart with my mother and father, to my father's village. My mother then left, and I sat down with my father and I started to cry and cry. The next day I asked where my mother was, and my father told me he was sorry she had had to leave but that she was coming back soon. She came back a few days later with her friend and she asked me why I was crying, but I could not explain that I was so frightened. She had to carry me everywhere she went because it was still hard for me to stand. My sister wanted to play with me but I couldn't walk. Once, when she threw the ball towards me, I fell down as I was so weak.

Later my mother took me to Gweru as she was worried that I was going deaf. She had called me several times but I hadn't replied, so she wanted to take me to find another doctor to check me. After examining me, the doctor told my mother that I was now deaf, that I could hear no sounds any more. The doctor said it was almost certainly because I had been so sick. My mother was desperate, and took me to the Johane Masowe church. We went inside, sat down and started to pray. We both prayed and prayed, but nothing happened and my hearing did not come back.

We stayed on in Gweru and eventually heard about another girl who was deaf who stayed near us. She could write and school was easy for her. The girl's mother explained everything to my mother and she started to look for a place for me in the Jairos Jiri Association Naran Centre. My mother had to find money for me and sort things out so that I could go to the school. As we arrived there I saw deaf school children signing, raising their hands as if they wanted to hit me. I touched my mother's hand and she told me not to be afraid. She told me these children are the same as you, but I was still afraid of the children. The headmaster said I should start in Grade Zero because I didn't know sign language, despite my mother telling him that I had been in Grade 4. There the teacher asked me 'What is your name?' and I wrote it down very quickly. The teacher realized that I had been sent to the wrong class and I went back to Grade 4. Everyone was surprised, and I was so pleased when I then passed all my subjects.

At that time my mother started to become very ill. One day an ambulance took her to hospital and they called my sister to go with her. I was left with my father and they told me about my mother but I didn't understand how serious it was because I was deaf. She was discharged and went to stay with my aunt. A short while later my mother died, but they did not tell me, they just told me to go and play with my cousins. My aunt came and took me to the village. When I asked my aunt, she told me that my mother was fine. When we got to the village I ran to my sister as I had brought chips to give my mother. But my sister told me that my mother was still in hospital. She didn't want to tell me that my mother was dead, they were all afraid to tell me because they knew that I would scream. So I kept the chips for my mother. The next day I met a boy who wrote down that I should go to the foot of the nearby mountain and that I would find my mother buried there. I nearly collapsed, I cried and cried and I asked my aunt why she hadn't told me. She responded that she was sorry and that I should forgive her, but I was so upset that she had told me lies. I never did see my mother's body. I took a stone and put it on the grave and I cried and I cried because my mother was dead and I had been told so many lies. Later my father also died and there was no happiness in my life. I cried a lot for a long time after that, sometimes pretending to others that I was happy and smiling.

I now live in Chibi growth point with my aunt. I have got two older sisters and one older brother, and we are all doing well. I am happy at school, my favourite subjects being accounts, computer studies, English, food preparation, mathematics and agriculture.

Taking Nature for Granted

Arthur Dzowa

God gave us freedom to choose. Choose who to talk to, who to love, what to do and what not to do, but did He promise that He would be responsible for the outcome? Go to a party and get drunk, fight with friends, take drugs, don't take school seriously – who will be responsible for the outcome? Is it God?

Too much of anything is not good. Perhaps God gives us too much freedom. Choose between tradition and Christianity, choose what to eat, choose between modern medicine and traditional medicine, traditional healers versus medical practitioners. They say in life never say never. Should people use both or stick to one. Do they really stick to their choices or does it depend on how bad the matter is.

The HIV virus is a menace these days. Traditional healers claim that they can treat it. Medical personnel say they can only control it. HIV/AIDS is like a bus travelling on a public road. A bus picks up passengers and these passengers become part and parcel of the bus. If the bus in involved in an accident, passengers also suffer. So it is with HIV/AIDS. If you let it into your body it will pick any disease that you are exposed to and these diseases become part of you.

Some of its favourite passengers are tuberculosis, cancer, pneumonia, meningitis and diarrhoea. So it you decide to follow the modern way you may control the virus but the virus may invite its friends in. Once inside, who will be responsible, modern medicine, you or God? On the other hand traditional healers use herbs, parts of animals and some form of magic that they claim scares the virus away. This is what I gathered from my dear grandfather.

So the choice is yours. Use nature or technology and be responsible for the choice.

Disabled but Happy

Sakhile Ndlovu

Born disabled
Born in God's image
We are human beings like others
Disabled does not mean not able
Some of us cannot stand, but we are happy
Some of us cannot run, but we are happy
Surely God created us for a purpose?
Everything God does has a reason.

God sees us in his own image
Some see us otherwise
But we are still happy.
Disabled does not mean poor
The way you do it, I can do it too
The way you cannot do it, I too cannot
Our uniqueness is God's creation.

God cares for us, watches over us everyday
Guides, comforts and lightens the way.
Education cannot change the human mind
Attitudes have been developed over the years.
Change – for you do not know your destiny.
I did not choose who I am, I am special.
Change – it will begin with you
Then it will flow like waters
From Galilee into the Jordan River.

A Bully Boy

Lloyd Nhapata

Once upon a time, in Zimbabwe, in the capital city of Harare, lived a great big boy named Tatenda. The young man bullied his two younger sisters and his brother. He often took their lunch and ate it. Tatenda also forced his sisters and brother to carry him and his bag to school. One would carry his bag, and the other two would carry him. Whenever they refused doing as Tatenda wished, he threatened cutting their little heads off. In fear, the little boy and girls carried Tatenda and his bag.

Each time they were about to get to school, Tatenda would take his bag and carry it himself. He did not want anyone to realise that he was bulling the younger children. On getting to class, Tatenda's brother and sisters would fall asleep. They did poorly in school as they were so tired. When their teachers asked why they did not do better, the little children were afraid to say anything. They were so scared of Tatenda.

Tatenda would take and eat the younger ones' lunch. They were then hungry, and in turn would go on and steal the lunch of their classmates. The classmates would then report them to the teacher on duty, and Tatenda's brother and sisters were often punished.

Upon coming back from school, the bully Tatenda would force his brother and sisters to wash his school-uniform, polish his shoes and write his homework. He ordered them to write all he told them; this they did every day. One teacher, Mrs Moyo, began to notice the ill-treatment. She telephoned the children's parents and asked them to come to school. They arrived at the school just thirty minutes after Mrs Moyo's phone call.

Tatenda the bully was then called to the headmaster's office. Mrs Moyo, the headmaster and Tatenda's parents were all there. The young man initially denied that he had been abusing the little children, but the adults didn't believe him. Eventually, Tatenda admitted that he had been wrong in what he had done to his brother and sisters. He promised his parents and the teachers that he would never do it again. Tatenda told the children that he was sorry and asked them to forgive him. The children he had troubled were finally free.

Broken-Hearted

Gary Vundhla

When I remember the good times we once had
I find myself in an empty street
Where I'm in a war with my heart, forever letting you go
I wish I had seen it coming but it is said
If wishes were horses beggars would ride too!

You promised me that you would never leave me
Comforted me and said this love is unbreakable
I even defined this love unconditional
But I was so wrong for so long
For thinking this love would never end.

Did you leave me because of my wrong deeds?
If so, I'm only human
Sometimes I make mistakes.
I wish that you were here with me
And I could see you once again,
Share the good old days
The promises we made
That this love would last forever.

Today I'm a broken-hearted girl
In an empty house
Lonely and sick at heart.
I should have read the signs
So I could have hoped and prayed harder
That those things between us would get better
But I guess it's over.

Nature Talks

Natasha Masumba

As I walked through the forest, I kicked stones, grasses and small creatures that crawled on the ground. I looked at the different levels of the veld. What a wonder: thorny bushes, rough barks, pointed leaves, round leaves, purple flowers, red flowers, pink flowers, flowers of all colours; all beautiful and of different shapes.
I started singing my favourite rhyme from Early Childhood Development:

> Colours, colours, colours
> Red is a colour
> Blue is a colour
> Purple is a colour

I began to collect flowers of different colours and shapes. As I approached a rose bush, it was not as friendly as the rest. It had beautiful flowers but not so easy to get. I looked at it, talked to it gently and picked a red rose. Next to it was a pink one, so I had to use the same technique on all the roses.

I moved on to the snot apple tree, it had fruits but they were hard and dry. They call it Mutohwe in Shona or Xakuxaku in Ndebele. I took the fruit, but was it of any use being hard and dry? I threw it away. But why, just because it looked different? I ran back and picked it up, apologizing quietly I threw it in my collection.

This made me think about my family. We live in Mahatshula suburb. My mother is not well because she is HIV positive. It does not show but she talks about it openly. Our neighbours do all they can to help. These neighbours are not positive but they treat us as equals. I was born with the disease. My teacher knows about it and she comforts me when I am not well. I also try to educate my friends about the disease.

What I have realized is that HIV/AIDS does not make us any different from the rest. At school I know of five teachers who are also positive. We sometimes meet when we go to collect our supplies. One of them told me that she was born with it and now she is thirty-five years old. This gives me hope.

HIV and AIDS pricks as a rose bush but does not change you. You remain as beautiful as a rose flower. It makes people slightly different, like the snot apple, but you still remain part of the community. People who are positive need love and affection just like everyone else. We are all God's creations. The disease will not affect the way people talk, think or act. It is not spread through air, food or water. So be educated and informed, and don't discriminate against HIV positive people. We are part of the community, the virus lives inside our bodies, not around us.

Biographies

Arthur Dzowa, thirteen years old and in Form 1. I am an only child and I live with my mother. I love soccer, watching movies and writing stories.

Elisha Gumbo. I am a boy who is inspired and motivated by education. I respect and honour humanity and nature because they were created.

Tanatswa Gwetsai. I am fourteen years old, in Form 1. I love caring and supporting my friends.

Thandazani Khoza, a very quiet girl, but very talented. I believe in myself and hope to be a successful singer and songwriter one day.

Michelle Mabaleka, a girl aged twelve. I am currently in Grade 6. I love singing and writing poems.

Ocean Maidza. Crazy, intelligent, adventurous and seventeen years old. My ambitions are to be either a lawyer or an accountant, but they say that all study with no play makes Jack a dull boy. I am a wheelchair tennis player and also play marimba.

Tsitsi Marenga. I am a girl aged eleven, currently in Grade 6. In my family we are five. During my spare time I like to read novels, especially those written by Kelly Johnson.

Sarah Mareni, in Form 4 at KGVI. I am really keen to do well in school and to be successful in life so that I can help my family and others too.

Natasha Masumba, born into a loving family with a lot of potential. It has always been my wish to spread my wings and see the world.

Chipo Mazodze. I am fifteen years of age. I am an intelligent girl who believes that if you work hard you can achieve anything in life.

Marvelous Mbulo. My life is a beautiful and inspiring story, it teaches me to never give up. Listen to the sound of my pen for a moment and read my story. I am a writer.

Mduduzi Mlotshwa, aged thirteen, a strong and handsome boy. I like eating rice with everything and my favourite sport is football.

Vimbai Mucheriwa. I am a person with a very, very huge imagination. My mind is filled with a lot of wonders beyond anyone's expectations.

Calvin Mwinde. Born and raised by a good, loving and caring family, I am full of potential and talent. Proud of being imaginative and adventurous.

Abigail Ncube, a girl of fourteen in Form 1 at King George VI. I love tolerance and motivating others, but hate gossiping.

Precious Sibanda. My dream is to be famous and glamorous. I want to be a star and see the world.

Primrose Ndlovu. I try not to dream but to live my dream because I am optimistic about life and believe that everything is possible.

Sakhile Ndlovu, a girl with confidence, aged thirteen. I am a close observer of nature.

Lloyd Nhapata. I am aged thirteen, the last born in a family of five. I really like to be at school and to read novels in my pleasure time.

Alex Nyathi. I was born with a number of challenges and turned to a love of nature for moral and social support.

Oleander Payarira, a TV fanatic but organised. I always try to relate what I see to real life situations. Being positive is my motto!

Preferment Rupondo, a girl aged twenty-one. Though physically challenged I am intelligent and I believe that success comes through hard work.

Gaudencia Rutize. I am a deaf girl with a passion to help deaf people achieve great things in life. I love dancing.

Alice Senda. I'm all about adventure and exotic food. I love people, socialising and want to know more about everyone.

Miyethani Sithole. I am deaf and have just completed my studies at King George VI. I did so well in my exams and am now studying cosmetology in Cape Town.

Paidashe Yolanda Tekede. I am deaf and clever, and my hands speak and write. I love writing and dancing.

Sininisabo Tshuma, an artist who tries to make a living selling my paintings. I create beauty, express fantasy and harmony, trying to stimulate the intellect and reflect a social and cultural context.

Gary Vundhla, a girl aged eighteen. I passed my 'O' levels in 2013 and am now in Lower 6th. I am a book worm and I also love socialising with everyone. I hate people who lie about me.

Anesu Zhira. I am a deaf boy who likes to play sports and communicate with other people.